Ghettostocracy

Oni the Haitian Sensation

Library and Archives Canada Cataloguing in Publication
Oni the Haitian Sensation
   Ghettostocracy / Oni the Haitian Sensation.

Poems.
ISBN 1-894692-17-9
   I. Title.
PS8629.N5G54 2006   C811'.6   C2006-905271-9

Editor: Dr. George Elliot Clarke
Copy Editor: S. Truhart
Cover Illustration: John W. MacDonald, series entitled Oni Warhol
Cover Design: Danilo McDowell-McCallum
Inside Layout: Heather Guylar

McGilligan Books gratefully acknowledges the support of the
Ontario Book Publishing Tax Credit for our publishing program.

To Issa, Anthony, Toussaint, I love you with all my heart;
to Marie Lucie Étienne Lucien (1919-1999),
Marlène Lucien, and to all of the single mothers in the universe.

Contents

III: Politricks 65

IV: Afromatrix 87

V: Poet Talks 99

Are You Experienced?

Oni, the Haitian Sensation, is the true one and only. She is utterly original to Anglo-Canadian poetics and to African-Canadian literature. Yeah, there are performance poets, Spoken Word poets, and Dub poets, and many of them are excellent (despite the deafness of old-school and Eurocentric critics to this outspoken art): but not one is like her; none is raw, as succinctly brassy, or as boldface sexy. Her closest avatars? Both are African-American 'vamps' (I use the term as praise): Wanda Coleman and Sapphire. (If ya ain't read these poets, get to it, bwoy; hop to it, gal!) But let's not leave out the Haitian-American artist Jean-Michel Basquiat – or the Haitian-Quebecois writer, Dany Laferrière: Oni shares with them a sense of exuberant satire, of being able to smile and spit in a jerk's eye simultaneously. (And don't you forget that Oni is a mighty fine artist – painter – too.)

These poems are courageously outrageous – and outraged – because Oni has experienced the outrages recorded herein: 'brothers' who just want to bed 'booty' and spurn the precious babies that are the natural, God-blessed result; cops – and 'gang-bangers' – all too trigger-happy (especially towards 'niggers'); urban dysfunction and fools-only-schools; country club racism and nightclub sexism; industrial terrorism poisoning our air, our water, our food and the enemies of poetry – this living, breathing art – exalting only what is long-dead and safely academic. To combat all such 'stupidness,' her rhymes drop into place like bullets from an AK-47; her imagery composes a bull's-eye.

To quote African-America's great rock guitarist, Jimi Hendrix, "Are you experienced?" The verses herein are not for virgin eyes and ears. Oni is one of those archetypal, black, women rebels – like Nanny-of-the-Maroons, or Harriet Tubman, or Marie-Joseph Angélique, Zenobia, or (hell, yes) *my* Aunt Joan – an unabashed truth-teller, *aware* of euphemisms but disrespecting all of *em*. These women are about gettin down to the nitty-gritty, talkin earthy, and tellin it like it is. Can you stand it? *Are you experienced?*

Ghettostocracy is an unforgettable book by an inimitable, drop-dead gorgeous *artiste.* Look out! These poems will make your nostrils flare, your pulse quicken, and your brain smarter...

George Elliot Clarke
E.J. Pratt Professor of Canadian Literature
University of Toronto
Laureate, 2001 Governor-General's Award for Poetry

Sak pasé moun mwen?

I

Growing up, it seems to me that if a white woman's identity is wrapped up in her weight, a black woman's identity is wrapped up in her hair. Yet, growing up in Ottawa, it seemed that Black people do not have a place in history other than being American slaves. We have Black Royals: Queen Charlotte, wife of the English King George III (1738-1820), was directly descended from Margarita de Castro y Sousa, a Black branch of the Portuguese Royal House. She is the grandmother of Queen Victoria, and the great-great-great-great-grandmother of the current Queen of the United Kingdom, Queen Elizabeth II. Queen Philippa, England's first Black Queen, Mother of the Black Prince, *Édouard le Noir*, the Prince of Wales (1330-1376). All of these people are now bleached or obscured; we have our own Black Queen, Her Excellency, Michaëlle Jean, Governor General of Canada, sworn to the Queen's Privy Council for Canada. I hope that they do not paint her white in the history books.

"This be the repercussion of the Black voice –
to be dark ivy vying against marble tombs."

- George Elliott Clarke

II

I come from a long line of naturally Black Haitian poets. My parents were born in Jérémie, "The City of Poets," and birthplace of the father of Alexandre Dumas, author of *The Three Musketeers*. Arawak, Queen Anacaona, ruled Hispaniola, Haiti and the Dominican Republic, with poetry. I emerged onto the international poetry scene as a teenager when I studied fashion arts on a varsity badminton scholarship from Seneca College in Toronto. My grandmother told me that I was protected. As a young lady I was convinced I was invincible, and that nothing could happen to me: I felt fabulous and strong, yet I was extremely vulnerable. I was not sure how to be me.

"A bird doesn't sing because it has an answer, it sings because it has a song."

- Maya Angelou

Before my studies were over, I found myself with child, and without my college degree. I discovered that poverty and a lack of education affects your health more than smoking, and that too many women on this planet are left with the responsibility of caring for children on one income – without receiving child support. (I want to thank my mother for putting me through school; I'm glad I've graduated, twice, and I hope to make it 'thrice,' be 'DR.,' me.) One in five women in Canada lives in poverty – that's 2.8 million women. Non-payment of child support is one of the greatest causes of poverty… it's time for revolution! (I have never received any child support payments from my sperm donors: respectively, a poet affiliated with The Last Poets, and from Bin-shooting-and-looting-no-cock-tax-paying-AP, from South Central LA: I want my money from both of these *biatches* who owe it to me; pass the message! Sisters give away too much free pussy: we need to get paid!) I am the Queen of Spades.

"Life is too short to make just one decision; God is too big for just one religion."   **- Michael Franti**

Poverty caused by lack of child support payments is becoming a major epidemic that society is ignoring. We should all have the right to a healthy and balanced life, and our children should have the same chance at a better future as any child on this planet. This is quite hard to do when you are constantly trying to decide between paying rent and buying groceries.

"Hold fast to dreams, for if dreams die, life is a broken winged bird that cannot fly."   **- Langston Hughes**

Ghettostocracy was written between Ottawa, Gloucester, Toronto, Scarborough, Montréal, New York, Nantes, Los Angeles, Düsseldorf, and Brisbane. In 1997, I lived in Crip Territory, with a *Canadien* accent, in South Central Los Angeles (by accident), surrounded by hood rats, and by the *baddest mahfuckers* I have ever met, five years after the Los Angeles Riots… with a partial post-secondary educa-tion; with one child on my arms, one in my belly… the year Biggie Smalls and Betty Shabazz died, one year after Tupac Shakur died, the year Geronimo Pratt was released from prison, and the year my second child was born…

"My uncle's dying wish was to have me sitting on his lap. He was in the electric chair."   **- Phil McCracklin (Grayling)**

IV

I grew up between Ottawa, Montréal, Toronto, New York, and Los Angeles. I first heard of South Central LA from listening to NWA, JJ Fad, and from *Boyz N The Hood*. I had no idea that I was moving to South Central – until I got there – what a culture shock!

Yo… every night there were snipers on the roof of my apartment: shooting every night… I was "commando crawling" in the Wild Wild West, when I was eight-months pregnant, dodging bullets: in my hood, there were more prison buses than school buses.

One of the highlights of my stay in Los Angeles was meeting Angela Davis. Los Angeles was trippy: luxury on one side, war and major poverty on the other…

The dude I lived with in Los Angeles was a nutter. He threatened to kill me if I left him. I escaped from his crazy ass! Now I am here to give you my poetry.

"I'm not here to say that every African-American descendant of slaves should receive 40 acres and, I guess now, a SUV. That should not happen. But there should be some compensation for those who are bottom-stuck by virtue of people who have been enslaved and then second-class citizens have to go through."
                                        - Johnnie Cochran

V

George passed me my second edit of *Ghettostocracy* during High Tea with his daughter, Aurélia, at Ottawa's Château Laurier. I first met George Elliott Clarke while he launched *Whylah Falls* on Parliament Hill, December 16th 1990. He blew me away. George was the first person I ever saw sweat and pulsate while reciting poetry, and his poem, *Love Letter to an African Woman*, in the First Edition of *Whylah Falls*, on page 58, made *mi tun fool*… I wanted to be like George when I grew up. George is very handsome, eloquent, real, and proudly Black. George's poetry made me feel beautiful as an Africadian woman. He has been a positive influence on my life and my writing since that day, and *I luv he more dan cook food*. I'm so blessed to have George as a mentor.

"Education is a progressive discovery of our ignorance."
- Will Durant

VI

My first poetry performance was in Toronto at the Bickford Auditorium in 1992, with *The Young Poets of the Revolution*, organized by MACPRI. The Toronto International Dub Poetry Festival was the first festival I ever performed in. As a poet, I have worked on three continents, promoting Spoken Word poetry locally and globally, and I directed Canada's first National Slam poetry competition, "The Canadian Spoken Wordlympics," *with almost no bling*.

"Un pour tous et tous pour un."　　　**- Alexandre Dumas**

VII

I have been through many incarnations in my life as a poet: I am a rap poet, a beat poet, a spoken word poet, a dub poet, a rock poet, a jazz poet, a blues poet, a sound poet, a punk poet, a slam poet, a spoken word poet. *"Poet"* is a strong common denominator in my life.

I want to thank my wonderful sons Issa, Anthony, and Toussaint for making me a better mom, a better person. *Mammy vous aime beaucoup*, you beautiful little men. Poetry has been extremely therapeutic… I'm hopelessly devoted to poetry. It has given to me what is refused to so many of us: freedom of imagination, freedom of speech.

"People see God every day, they just don't recognize him."
- Pearl Bailey

Oni the Haitian Sensation
South Central Ottawa, Ontario
August 2006

1: Ghettostocracy

"Ghetto" means poverty stricken urban area +
"Cracy" means to rule, to hold sway = Ghettostocracy.

Ghettostocracy consists of the nobility
or ruling classes of the Ghetto.

Ghettostocracy

(Hook)
Ghettostocracy, created by hypocrisy,
Is an ideology
That can never set me free.
Look at me!
Poetry is the tool that set me free.
It you feel me, count to three.
No apology: my history.

Introducing the Duchess of Work: not a bureaucrat, but a
ghettoristocrat full of crap.
(Soulful voice...)
My crack pipe is a call to arms; you don't bother me: I brave a
society of scars. When the wind blows, I go to work...
Ghettostocracy.

(Hook)

Introducing the Queen of Spades: she has three-baby daddies and
she never gets paid.
(Raspy voice...)
I am a knave in a court of law. I am welfare's property, and I keep
food stamps in my bra.
I have no future, so let me sleep.
Ghettostocracy.
(Hook)

Introducing the Duke of Danger: he lives in a jail cell where
strangers don't stay strangers.

(Tyrannical voice...)

I had nice clothes and mad dollar bills. I smoked another brother
to give myself a thrill.
What have I done? I'm too young to die.
Ghettostocracy.

(Hook)

Introducing the King of Hardcore: he claims to be rich, but he is mad poor.
(Boastful voice…)
I skip school to show unskilled cool. I am uneducated; therefore, an ideal bughouse-fool.
I punished myself so I lost my wealth.
Ghettostocracy.

Introducing Reverend Seymour Cash: he just raped the ghetto to escape into the upper class.
(Silky voice…)
I was a pimp, now I'm a man of God. Give me your cash money; I have to do my job.
I mean, your shot-or-stabbed ass is goin down in an early grave!
Ghettostocracy.

Introducing the Princess of Pain: she wears white panties and don't care bout her stains.
(Jazzy voice…)
I have no home, but I own a comb. I live in a cardboard castle, concretely alone. Where are my forty acres and my mule?
Ghettostocracy:
Home of hip-hop hypocrisy…

Baby, It's Cold Outside

When an artist
Walks on Jarvis,
She works the hardest…

Greetings from the Dirty White North!
Baby, it's cold outside, it's cold outside,
As I slip on ice sheet streets,
Paved concaved and convex from the skids paved
By people crazed like goons at a hockey game,
Trying claim to fame…

Baby, it's cold outside, it's cold outside.
Baby, it's cold outside, it's cold outside.

Blizzards of people, cold-fronted, chilled by reality,
Penguin suits for jobs, natural hair robbed.
Replaced by permafrost perms –
Cool Afros burned to grow "with the flow."

Baby, it's cold outside, it's cold outside.
Baby, it's cold outside, it's cold outside.
As I write to you from my igloo,
My icy point-of-view is crystal clear.
When I say that ice cream dreams are melted away,
Chocolate chips dip and die doing death-defying deeds,
Doing dope to cope on ski slopes,
With million dollar skis to make their feet look sweet.

Baby, it's cold outside, it's cold outside.
Baby, it's cold outside, it's cold outside.
"Let it snow, let it snow, let it snow."
Snowmen shooting snowballs on black ice,
Gangsters on dialysis,
Travel in twos, killing spades on skidoo.
I sing the blues, I sing the blues, I sing the blues.
I have the wind power to cope

With ice-fox toms cooling off at Caribana,
Drinking *Tropicana*,
As I think of the ROM,
As I think of the ROM,
As I think of the ROM...

Baby, it's cold outside, it's cold outside.
Baby, it's cold outside, it's cold outside.
Cold-hearted people will not work together –
Despite the bad weather.
Cold cash in the city: that freezing black economy
Means bankruptcy for we.
Instead of we working collectively,
In the vein of creativity,
Effectively, Jack Frost, the big Black boss,
Told me to get lost in the cold.
My melted dreams made me scream and scheme
As frostbite burned my cold cash, cold as ice cream.

Baby, it's cold outside, it's cold outside.
Baby, it's cold outside, it's cold outside.
Waiting outside the club, snubbed,
While others dance to rub-a-dub-dub
I'm without –
A frozen hair weave to dance to dub.

A fudgecicle-fine brotha passes by.
I say: "Hi," and he disses me to frolic in the white snow.
He melts in the ice queen's cold front.
That's cold....
Baby, it's cold outside, it's cold outside.
Baby, it's cold outside, it's cold outside.

That cold Canuck, *Out of Africa* exhibit, back in the early '90s, in the T-Dot, at the Royal Ontario Museum, that portrayed Africans as savages, white Canadians as saints, when the Africans were proud warriors resisting Canada's undiagnosed imperialism.

California Dreamin

The pollution in Los Angeles has
Occupied the Californian sky.
Its stars fell out of the stratosphere
Of the Western Hemisphere:
Hollywood stars
Scintillated on the ground after sundown.

It was not quiet
Five years after the riots.
Florence and Normandy,
Compose Ghettostocracy.
Sweet-fleshed children play:
Predators glance their way.
Trash steams and stinks up the streets,
Beneath Hollywood's heat.
Beverly Hills butts on the horizon
Of murder, abuse, prostitution,
Living-dead living conditions,
Human survival, rivals, and
Urban revival, plus dapper devils.
Lights! Cameras! Action! A thong!
Urban nomads drive chromed shopping carts
While junkies are jiving redemption songs.
Drunks do the jig, rumors get big,
Suicidal is the norm,
So is kiddy porn.
Politicians get kicks
After the Quiet Storm
The preservation of the environment is no longer a popular trend.
On a polluted day, I cannot recognize LA.
In 2025, water will end.
Blue gold, black blues.
Black gold, blue balls.
California dreaming
Has a meaning
When the Pacific Ocean falls

Behind Hollywood.
Seismological uproar
Brings
Torrential action on city shores.

Black widows and buzzards
Fear the *Dukes of Hazzard*.
General Lee and *Sara Lee*
Eat crumpets with their tea.
Confederate flags and doo rags
Accentuate your body bag.

The Los Angeles Riots began in 1992 at the intersection of Florence and
Normandy. I lived ten blocks away from where the riots began five years
after the Los Angeles Riots took place.

"The Quiet Storm" was the name of a Soul music radio show that came on
late at night. During my stay in Los Angeles, I was sequestered in a tiny room
and I spent many hours listening to "The Quiet Storm" on the radio.

California's justice system was created on confederate values, even though
the state is actually named for a Black woman.

Gangster Alliance

Fourteen days of death in the fall of 2002
In South Central LA,
Plus the Bloody Weekends in Toronto,
Made me want to blast these verses
For the steery-eerie-eerie-o:

Peace to Merlin Santana!
Here today, and gone *manana*...
Inner city war zones
Not in Iraq, not caused by Al Capone.
Twenty shots, beat downs,
In suburban and in urban towns.
Rash of violence + silence =
Gangster alliance.

Three strikes, and you're in:
Thanks to guilty conscience, but sweet, sweet sin.

The "Three Strikes" law jails your ass for life after you are convicted 3 times
for crimes.

Ghetto Champagne

Pancakes, no syrup.
Kool-Aid; no sugar.
Bread – no butter.
Babies, no daddy.
Fridge, no food.
Car, no gas.
Wings, no hot sauce.
Cookout, no food.
Pimp, no bling.
Tits, no ass.
Skirt, no panties.
Cell phone, no charger.
Rice, no peas.
Beer money, champagne thirst.
Ghetto Champagne.

Sixty

Six times ten, murdering foes and friends,
Caused my hood's demise:
Ghettostocracized...
All go to
Jail without a doubt.
With hazy eyes,
Machine-washable bloodstains
On *Sean John* jeans:

Gang life, prison wife, without *Vaseline*.

Hilfiger kill a niggah:
Jheri-Curls fried like fritters.
Bodies disposed like kitty litter...

Death row, low blow,
Life starts at zero.
Hero with an ego,
Gets emcee material
Of jailhouse rock,
Prosti-tots,
Pus-infected cocks.
Legislation perpetuates the problem:
Those who suffer are the ones who can't solve them.
Big up, grassroots!
Stomping streets in your big black boots.
But you ain't got no loot.
No, you ain't got no fruit.
What a catastrophe!
In the land of the free,

Roll call...listen y'all:
Absent fathers – in jail,
Absent mothers – in jail,
Absent sons – in jail,
Absent daughters – in jail.

Is it that much fun to fail?
High school dropouts,
Join gangs, then chain gangs, no doubt.
(Yeah, chain gang without a doubt.
And when you bend over, watch out!)

Poverty and criminality
Reinvent slavery!
My ancestors are in the sea:
It's my duty to stay free.

Nasty Drunk Funk

Hit me,
One time!
Head space,
No mind.
Awww…
Typical deal:
Potential,
Cars,
No wheels!
Dance on the tables –
With no shoes,
To funk, to blues.
Clap!
Slap that ass!
We killed the bed,
It bled.
Hurt me,
You're dead!
Get down, on time,
Quit playing games with my mind.
Rewind!
Nasty drunk,
What's up?
What's in your cup?
Funk?
Snapshots, in time,
8-track, rewind.
Wander, from place to place
Reality?
Taste.
Do it yourself,
Can't be alone,
Make your bottle your home.
Spin the bottle:
Flip it!
Sip it!

Dip it!
What's what?
What's in your cup?
Say it loud:
Proud on a cloud,
Play the punk.
Rock – my boat
Your periscope is filled with coke
Ooooww.

Have You Walked In These Shoes?

Have you ever walked outside barefoot in the snow,
Calling those who love you most your biggest foes,
Refusing to rationalize the truth before you,
Mistaking unconditional love for the phrase 'I adore you'?

Have you ever seen the base of your foot bleed
From sliding on broken glass, while you're skidding
Downhill to poverty from the middle-class?
Have you had a masked friend uproot you
From the ecosystem that should salute you?

Have you ever been transplanted to a new nest,
While carrying a new lump under your chest?
The lump alone had skin and bones
And took nine months to rest.

Have you ever shopped without having money?
Has fashion ever seemed *Beverly Hillbillies*-funny?
If designer sense made small change,
Then dollar bills and chills
Would chill out on chains.

Have you ever looked into a mirror with dopey eyes?
Have you heard a mirror swear that you're living a lie?

Frankie And Joanie Blues

She don't itch –
Cause she got it scratched.
Some people act free
Though they're supposed to be attached.
Joanie didn't keep her legs shut
Cause he didn't keep em open.
Frankie didn't take care of his girl
When he was sittin on top of the world.
Joanie said:
"What would you do if Frankie didn't take care of you?"

She don't bitch cause
She got herself a bone.
When Joanie was in the doghouse,
Frankie began to roam.
Frankie didn't take care of business
And his whole world fell apart.
Have you ever witnessed
The pulverizing of a cracked-up heart?
She don't snitch.
She don't care.
She don't think that life
Handles her with care.
Joanie needs an angel
Who understands what's goin on…
Every vinyl record
Is two-faced –
Like a sexual-freedom song.
She don't twitch;
Joanie can barely stand.
She can't repair any glitch
With a broken hand.
Frankie bust her hand
In a tiff, a rage.
When his show was over,
He left the stage.

Frankie wrote Joanie a poem
With his cocked bone.
And he tattled a nasty tome
On her gramophone:

I never loved you, bitch,
And now I broke your heart.
Bitch, I despise all of you –
And you'll never get a brand new start.
Imagine me in happy land,
While tears stain your pillow.
When I killed your other man
Ha! – I pissed on his shadow.

Joanie needed to stitch
Her now-imaginary heart.
Life begins with imagery
That hell tries to take apart.
Joanie was alone
With a gramophone –
When winter warped her mind
And her heart froze to stone.

Frankie's fucking hatred
Stuck a stake in her heart.
Joanie felt like a mistake.
She took herself apart.

He did not "sex her"; therefore she had to find another lover. Frankie did not "dig" polyandry.

Tales From The Hood

Crips with whips and high-top fades
Become bullet-ridden marmalade.

Or they pour libation, day by day,
Malt liquor that mocks Africa.
Ricochet, falsetto cry –
Do you have an alibi?
Six-six-six, six-six-six,
Designer crucifix, hood flicks,

Ghetto golliwogs go agog
Get heart attacks living high on hog.

Fetus-flavored jelly,
Cakes made in her belly,
Micro-waved live, dumplings die.
Chicken wings fry
On *Betty Crocker* jive.
Pablum makes spaghetti
Into crack cocaine confetti.

Gwen

I had a suicidal friend named Gwen.
Gwen said she enjoyed life,
But I said: "Gwen don't pretend!"
OK, her real name really wasn't Gwen.
She was a friend, from way back when.

Gwen and I had an eye for fashion.
I wore bangles, Gwen slit her wrists.
OK, now, what should be my reaction?
Stupefaction! So I'll tell it like it is.

Gwen quit school and played the fool.
Thinking her body was her only tool.
Gucci bags, stereotypes,
Crazed by magazines at seventeen:
She believed the hype!

Gwen thought a blow job meant breezy employment,
She worked double shifts for enjoyment.
Minimum wage was won between her legs.
Show a little cash, and Gwen would beg.

Gwen painted her face with caramel and fudge.
Her cherry-stained lips never had a smudge.
Belly had a pudge, she hardly ever budged.
She held a big grudge if her beauty was misjudged.

Gwen and I met guys named Stan and Sam
Stan was fly, Sam was mine, Stan was her man.
Gwen was fine not refined, she had a plan –
To become the concubine of Stan and Sam.

Gwen and I had an eye for men –
If I checked one, Gwen checked ten.
Gwen never really acted like a friend,
So I never ever talked to Gwen again.

I had a suicidal friend named Gwen.
Gwen said she enjoyed life,
But I said: "Gwen don't pretend!"
Ok, her real name really wasn't Gwen.
She was a friend: R.I.P., Gwen.

Elocution

Elocution: to speak out.
If you have a tale to tell –
Tell the tale and tell it well: prevail.

Elocution-Expression:
Feeling enthusiasm,
Orgasms, back spasms…
I think that I have had them when I practice – elocution.

Illiteracy-dysfunction, I-L-L-I-T-E-R-A-C-Y: Why?
How do you expect to "know thyself"
If starved of alphabet soup?
If you got no culture, you can't stage no coup.
What? Got no degree?
Then shut the fuck up, G!
And we do forget our culture.

Illiteracy fosters Ghettostocracy.
When your mama sends her kid to school
And he comes out a first-class fool,
And mama can't even read the damn, no-good diploma,
What trauma!

Illiteracy-fallacy.
See Dick walk. See Jane run.
Jane dicking Dick is fun.
But don't you feel like a dick,
When Dick and Jane are reading real quick,
And you can't even write – 'sick!'

Illiteracy – a problem.
Children in grade five can't read,
And they go to school indeed.
No homework done –
Nintendo is number one!
Where's mommy? Where's daddy?

Well... they're not at the library.
Illiteracy-tragedy.

Illiterate children in high school
Sucking teacher's dick to get through.
Shortly, they are on their way to college-acknowledged.
Some get raped and graduate,
Then become head of state.
But ask them, if they can spell the word 'potato'...
"P-O-T-A-T-O-E?"
I don't think so!!!
How do ya spell 'ho'?

Illiteracy-elocution-solution.
Say it loud, "I'm black and I'm proud."
Illiteracy in my community should not be allowed:
For those of us who need documented history,
To know who be part of we.
Hooked on phonics, symbiotic, using methods electronic.
To learn and to earn –
Knowledge is true power.
Literacy is-Power-Literacy is-Power-Literacy is…
Power!
Power!
POWER!
Black Power!

Dan Quayle's moment of embarrassment. He can't spell 'potato.' William
Figueroa, 12, was the boy who knew how to spell 'potato' even though
Quayle insisted on adding an 'e' to the end of the word during a US Vice
Presidential event.

Harlem...

Harlem...
Is my favorite place in this world.
'Tis where the woman left the girl.
Lennox Avenue and Malcolm X Boulevard,
Have sparked a chord from an erotic bard.
The renaissance is cyclic.
Revolutions go on.
Gyratory symbols, like Isis,
Have kissed my soul at dawn.
I was the Eve
My beginning
Had sprung in two's.
Harlem blues
Turned green.
The streets were mean.
I had a dream.
Harlem...
Had me walking on a cloud
Harlem...
Had me running off my mouth...
Harlem...
Was the most conducive place
Harlem...
Left a smile on my face.

New York Streets

I walk down the streets of the Big Black Apple with a rotten core:
Police, cops, walking the beat,
On their feet, in the streets,
Are beating big Black boys, with their toys.

Billy bats crack on their backs,
Shot dead in the head: As the posse members fled.
Red, red, blood flowing downtown –
From the East River's bed:
Drown!
During my stay,
I take the A-train from Rockaway.
Dollar cabs, downplay the avenues,
And then I'm on my way,
To Harlem, Street, 125,
I arrive, in daylight…
Dazzled, dangerous, and daring
Caring, I look at Black faces like mine,
Oh mine!
Winos sipping wine,
Bootleg tapes, and brothers oh so fine…
So I strut, with my big black butt, singing:
"Love is in the air,"
As I kiss my lover under the covers.
"Oh my love!"
I love Harlem, once a mecca,
Intense, with incense scents, seducing sexual sisters like me.
My analogy?
"Mercy, mercy, me," Marvin Gaye would say if he could see:
Senseless souls, seeking self, sniffing coke, smoking dope and
plea:
Guilty!
Cracked up cracked heads – crying crime.
Drum beats replaced by gunshots flexed in the head.
Brothers sucking dick,
Sisters doing tricks, getting sick, on their knees,

With disease, looking like blue cheese.
"NEW YORK! NEW YORK!":
"Start spreading the news, I'm leaving today, I wanna be a part of it,
NEW YORK! NEW YORK!"
Damn!
Van Wyck, makes me sick.
98.9, Kiss FM is fine.
Another cabbie got shot,
That happens a lot.
Jamaica, Queens, is my scene;
When I walk, I try to look mean.
I can't even look at my sister cos –
She thinks I want to kiss her,
So I diss her.
Stay Black, Stay Strong!
The Black Panthers are gone.
Black life is tragedy.
Houses look like jails; from the outside to the inside,
Like Rikers Island Hell.
Assata will tell you that it's
True.
Treacherous times, and torture telling lies.
The American Dream is mean;
It is made for the Right extreme.
As we feast in the belly of the beast, and decrease
From the feces in his butt crease…
Rest in peace on New York streets.

Assata Shakur was pulled over by the New Jersey State Police, shot twice and then charged with murder of a police officer. Assata spent six and a half years in prison under brutal circumstances before escaping out of the maximum security wing of the Clinton Correctional Facility for Women in New Jersey in 1979 and moving to Cuba. Source: http://www.assatashakur.org/

What Do You Say?

What do you say to a pregnant 11-year-old,
When she asks you if your gestation period is easy?
Do you scold her for being bold –
Or do you reprimand her for being sleazy?

What do you say when you see baby fat
And lactating breasts on a young girl?
Do you tell her that her life is ruined
Or do you simply compliment her tight curls?

What do you say to a little girl,
Who will soon be a mommy?
Do you share your wisdom with her,
Or do you tell her to put down her dollies?

When you ask her if she is having sex,
What do you say if she tells you, "No"?
What do you say when she tells you that her virginity,
Was given to someone who now calls her a hoe?

What do you say when she cries in your arms,
And asks you to take care of her and her baby?
Do you tell her that she is a big woman now,
And that she must begin to act like a lady?

When you find out that her dad is in jail,
And her mom is away with her new man?
Do you tell her to be responsible,
Or do you simply just say… "Damn"?

Being Poor Sucks

It sucks to be poor
Sometimes.
You are unsure of what you can endure –
Holes in your pockets,
Burned by a rocket,
Receding lines burned with poverty's fuel
It sucks being poor.

Eating each meal like it was your last,
Food in your fridge is a thing of the past,
Clothes worn and torn-fitting to last:

It sucks being poor.

Education is luxury behind closed doors,
Some get elevated, some clean dirty floors.
Hegemony and monopoly –
From shore to shore to shore to shore:

It sucks being poor.

A mari usque ad mare
From sea to sea to sea –
Rent money depletes in a hurry.
Stock-market nations mass-market poverty.
Makes me wanna holler, makes me want to roar.

It sucks being poor.

Naw, I'm not poor, "I'm financially impaired":
My riches lay in the stitches of my African flair.
Poor ladies look like witches – or rag-doll whores.
Uh-huh –
It sucks being poor –

Especially if you're a Moor
Frolicking with fewer *fuehrers* is one cure.

It sucks being poor.
It sucks being poor.

Stay

Why insist on leaving when you're barely breathing?
Stay with me awhile, sweet, suburban child.
Why pack up your luggage simply since you stopped bleeding?
Stay with me awhile baby, it's cold outside.
Please, don't leave my doors! Someone make her stay!
Don't cry on my floors: tears will make you sway.
Please, put on a coat! Someone bring her back!
I will always love you – even though you're a brat.
Someone, please stop her. I take back my words.
Please, don't leave, mommy's little girl.

I Am Not Ashamed To Say
That I Am In Pain

Last night I cried for the oppressed and the depressed.
My torrential tears, my copious, fast-descending tears,
Dilapidated my plentiful amount of *Kleenex*,
Leaving me perplexed.
Vexed, I grasped my black pen, put it in full effect, in retrospect –
Of the painful thoughts that clouded my head.
Instead of going to bed –
A brother is dead from a pig's lead.
His child needs to be fed; his family's left in the red.
He ain't done no wrong to nobody.
What about his family?

Morality?
Hah! Most police ain't got none:
Pulling triggers on a gun,
Aiming at the young (cause they think it's fun),
Having brothers on the run until their lives are done.
But one day, the pig will pay; he will be taken –
And fried like bacon.

Oh, you think I'm cruel now; it's like colonial rule now?
But GENOCIDE, INFANTICIDE
Assassinate my sense of pride.
I hate to see a mother crying –
Cos her baby lies dead in the cemetery –
His picture in the obituary, very, very, involuntarily,
Contrarily to those of us who strive to stay alive.
I am CRYING:
Can't you see that the race is dying?

Church

Church is like a party.
Church is like a party.
She came to church looking sexy, sexy,
Looking sexy for Jesus.
She even got baptized for him.
Church is like a party.
She came to church looking sexy, sexy.

What happened to the souls in dreamland,
Who went to church for The Word?

Church is like a party, party.
Don't come underdressed –
For the biblical wet-panty contest!

Church is a like a party, party.
Jesus preached in homemade sandals.
Now he'd be treated like an uncouth vandal.
Church is like a party, party.

The priest likes orgies, orgies.
Members of the clergy, clergy.
Feel very flirty, flirty.
Inducing virgins to adultery.
Church is like a party, party.
A party where you can take care of your spirit.
Instead some souls are just
A part of the gossip soul-train,
Created by jealousy,
Hidden by hypocrisy –
Sisters hustling pussy,
In the name of God!
They smile softly –
Then they stab you hard and good.
Church is like a party, party.
Where they judge you with open eyes.

Dub:

Dem gyal dem,
Up inna de church –
Sexy up demselves, for the sinistah ministah.
Dem gyal, dem,
Up inna de church –
Will thief your mon!
Amon!

Church is like a party, party.
Minister Seymour Cash –
Prime Ministah tap dat ass –
Dat mon deh – him a sinistah
The minister's mistresses –
Bounce on holy mattresses.

Church is like a party, party.
Mammary memories mess up mass
Message.
Most messengers miss it by not
Going to the church,
Just going to the party…
Church is like a party, party.

By Any Means Necessary!

(Mary Magdalena carries an empty wallet in her purse
To make one million meals.)

Feelin High

Could you please get me water; my mouth is dry:
You overdosed me with morphine, and I feel high.
You gave me morphine for my labor!
Please excuse my bad behavior –
This is the best I've felt since I've been here.
The medical staff
Overmedicated me while injecting my rear.
Opiates, not my cup of tea!
Am I a candidate for your experimental spree?
Hail Mary, full of grace –
Keep tears off my chubby face
My baby stopped moving,
Someone, help me please!
I'm boozing in the hospital,
And I feel like a sleaze.
My speech is incoherent like a wild current.
Why is this doctor adding to my torment?
My lament surely makes you laugh.
I am at your mercy because I have no cash.
You think I have no soul because I am dark,
If I was a dog, I would surely bark.
If I was a leper, I would surely beg.
If I was a drunk, I would drink a keg.
My speech has no control, this is why I babble
If this child leaves my body, he will have his rattle.
This is not what I expect from a maternity ward –
This room can be mistaken for the city morgue.

Santa Let His Afro Down

(Hook)

Santa let his Afro down. Parapapampam!
He came to my part of town. Parapapampam!
I heard his record play. Parapapampam!

God bless Jam Master Jay. Parapapampam,
Rapapampam, Rapapampam….
Ohhh, it's Christmas! What a bambam!
Send in the drums….

Santa let his Afro down, chillin with his shortie in my part of town.
He was sipping on a 40 with a ho – ho-ho – ,
And he dropped his red *Kangol* in the snow.
Christmas in the Pj's, Christmas in the hood.
Christmas in the ghetto, without cash, ain't good.
'Tis the season to be merry!
Spread joy by any means necessary!
(Hook)
Santa let his Afro down: you can say that he was an average clown.
He never wore a frown, he always wore a smile –
And his wayward reindeers were extra wild.
Rudolph did the running man, Dancer would pump up the jam,
Comet would wind up his waist, Vixen would turn up the bass.
(Hook)

Santa let his Afro down: he took his party to the Mercury Lounge.
Ottawa was set on fire, rocking with a funky yuletide choir.
Underneath the mistletoe, he kissed the ladies, row by row.
He was naughty… he was nice in the winter paradise:
Santa was a ladies' man and he had a wicked tan.
He used a lot of *Afro Sheen* and he wore designer jeans.
(Hook)
Santa had a lot of green: he drove a wicked limousine.

He went to a Kwanzaa party, in his cherry red *Ferrari*.
Santa used to be a pimp, now he changed his life around.
Santa used to be a blimp, now he slimmed his body down.
Santa took his cash money and he gave it to the poor.
Santa is a poetic hero, but Satan paints him a whore.
(Hook)

II: Love Hustle

The Dick You Need... A Lesson In Lexicology

The Dick you need
Is not a noun derived from the Latin word *testiculus*.
This is a test:
Testes are the Latin plural form of *testiculus*.
Testify!
This testament is a nut case.
A *testis* is a witness that resembles a pendulum.
Ding, dong!
Rise to the curriculum!

Wee men are "seamen":
Some men rock your boat,
Slip under your petticoat.
She sold seashells by the seashore
And she freaked,
When he raped her like a sea-bound whore.
 She was shell-shocked so she
 Kneed him in the gonads and fled.

Dick is a derivative of Richard.
You don't know Dick!
I mean, you don't know Richard.
A *dickey* fits snugly around your neck:
Moby Richard swims erect.
A *dickey* protects your neck:
The only dick you need is a dictionary.
My preference is reference.
The dictionary causes a positive mental interference.
Some dictionaries are small, while others have a wider appearance.
Some dictionaries are hardcover while others are paperback.
A thesaurus renders plural definitions,
Other dictionaries give you the hard facts.
Some dictionaries are well-defined;
Others will blow your mind.
Lexicographers are phonetic photographers –

Poets are stenographers.
Pragmatics define lyrical acrobatics.

Richards are polysemous;
Some have semen, some are serious.
The dictionary is the only Dick that you need.
Girlfriend, read!

Dirty 30's

The Great Depression was between her legs.
She needed a *New Deal*,
So she borrowed and she begged.
A little bit of money
Is all she needs.
Labor Unions rise between her thighs –
So does unregulated greed.
Once a month, her business cycle
Had a sticky price.
Her breasts were unemployed.
Now she thinks twice.

Love Letter To My Boo

If only I could re-arrange the alphabets, I'll put 'U' and 'I'
together.
Gurl, you so fine, gurl, I would like to get to know you better.
If you give me a chance, gurl, I'll try to make you mine.
Your curves are soft like puddin,
And you have the juiciest behind.
Gimme a chance, gurl.
You smell so pretty, your name must be Rose.
You're the only one I see when my eyes are closed.
I would eat you up like fried chicken by tasting your thighs and
breasts:
Gurl, gimme some sugah, I need you in my nest.
I would drink your bath water, and
I'd buy you a diamond-frosted car.
When you run through my mind, gurl, you erase every scar.
Gurl, you have beer money, but champagne taste.
My love for you is real, gurl, don't let it go to waste.
I love your nappy head, gurl. Damn gurl! You have good hair!
If you fry it like bacon, it would mess up your flair.
Please be my queen, gurl, I want to be your king –
I would hit the best pawnshop in town
To snatch your wedding ring.

Bitches In Ditches

Thou paper-faced, fod fat rabbit sucker,
Shake your hideous, shag-eared, clot pole.
Saucy bitches in ditches, mud-brained,
Hideous, evil-eyed, dog-hearted,
Lewd, wannabe whoresons, motley-minded
Hideous, eye-offending, soul creatures,
Piss off! Run mad, and addeth unmuzzled
Saucy, yeasty rump-fed, queasy, jaded lies,
And thou shalt have rank, empty-hearted bits
Of pernicious gruel between thou thighs.

Anon knavish kitty, let thyself go.
Thou purpled labia, rug-headed sow,
Knowest thy meaning of thy noun, 'hoe cake'
Let they self match visual imagery
That suits the true likes of thou raw-boned foe!
Thou wretch'd, roynish, onion-eyed lass,
Peevish-witted karma will kick thy fat ass!
Thou gnarling, drooling, shaved kitty cat growls
And combineth grace with mold on thy towel.
Thy pinch-spotted, jackanape stories are foul.

Hoedown

This... is...
My favorite poem, as you should know,
Twas written by a pimp for his hoe.
Twas written in the eighties, some time ago,
But why I love it, I just don't know.
Here goes...

The Hoe-down...

When we are so far apart,
Can sorrow break a tender heart?
I love you. I really do.
Sleep is sweet, I dream of you.
With this poem I had in mind,
You must read the first word in each line...

Twas written by a pimp, and this is true,
Who would beat his hoe black and blue.
And one day... the sun shone.
The hoe realized she was not alone.
The hoe became a ballerina, the pimp got a subpoena.
Then he learned to play the saxophone.
The hoe sat on a cloud and rained.
This thunderstorm imped the pimp's pain.

Out of this downpour bloomed a precious flower,
A faded rose for every hour.

This is my favorite poem, and it is true,
That a hoe can be a gentleman too.
Twas written by a pimp, and this is true.
This poem has one role: Mind control.
Now the pimp struts with a limp,
Because he could never buy the hoe's soul.

HOEDOWN...

HOEDOWN.
SHOWDOWN.
YEEHAW!

Making Scents

Could you be the one my heart beats for?
The one who will make me want no other?

Good heavens! Open the door!
Your putrescent scent has me on the floor,

How dare you come to the dance,
Without giving the shower a second chance?

Glance at me if you will,
My waters were running – and now they are still,
Stagnant. Your stench
Followed you here from the basketball bench.
Putrid foe! To think I thought of being your wench!

It is you I snub!
Perfume does not substitute for a shower –
It only makes a funky brother smell sour.
Fatal vision impossible!
May soap and water prove your apostle.
Your breath is a pistol –
So foul, I gotta blow the whistle.
My eyes grow dimmer as your aroma simmers.
And to think I once thought you were a winner!

Arrogance in this instance,
Makes no bloody sense!
Boy! The sistahs were not lying when they concluded
That you were intense –
And the only brother around here
Who made perfect scents!

I Knead Your Nuts

(This poem is a musical)

I knead your nuts.
I knead your nuts.
I knead your nuts.
I would eat the nuts off your sundae –
From Sunday to Monday, if you would only pay
Me more than peanuts and jelly beans, to provide your child's
means.

Your candy bar has melted; your nuts are in my hand –
Peanut butter smooth, like Peter Pan.
Nutty professor, **DNA** defender, you
Did
Not
Approve
An erotic groove, smooth like butter,
Or the milk out the udder.
Mind in the gutter –
Two-minute lover –

Stingy motherfucker, living a dream.
Loving your nuts, with cookies and cream.
Here's an *Oreo*, that's my story though –
In stereo:
 I'm a-rock this show slow…
 Tic-tac-toe,
 XXX,
 Let me flex –
 In the name of sex.
My eyes are enslaved:
They received lashes.
Ashes to ashes –
Take care of this package!

Nuts from the store,

Stolen like whores,
Peanut-butter brother,
I can't take it no more.
You're making my cherry
Go nuts, nuts, nuts,
Like very merry Mary –
Crazy for banana splits on butts.

Calling all squirrels!
Squirrels beware,
Make sure, make sure,
That the nuts you eat have no pubic hair!

Yesterday, a Blackman
Pulled a trigger –
It was his phallus –
And he shot me like a ni@@er,
The bullet holes in my womb were deep.
In nine months,
The resurrection had hands and feet.

This is nuts, this is true:
I ate your fucking nuts,
And now I'm black and blue.
True; this is from me to you:
Your nuts no longer put me in the mood.
Soul food –
Last meal –
Nuts in my basket, you know the deal.
Bust a nut –
Bust a rhyme –
Bust move and child-support payments on time!
The cotton you pick is the wool in my hair –
I'm a reflection of you: Why are you so fucking scared?
Keep yo nuts, give me the money.
Livin on welfare is not funny.

Honey turned into queen bee;

I'll stroke your nuts in the name of liberty.
Set me free with your nuts!
The seeds you breed gave me a big gut.
Your nuts and bolts is the subject of my revolt.
Man, I ate your pecan and it made me choke.
In the days of slavery, I rocked the boat.
Take me seriously, cause I ain't no joke!
If your nuts are an extension of your mind,
Don't you find that your third-eye is blind?

Rhythm is jism from a wet dream.
Reality is brutality from the right extreme.
Take it to the left in the name of theft,
Smoking black seeds like bootleg sess,
Black and blessed.
Bless the mic –
Your love is just as
Extreme as Tina and Ike…

Me so Oni, takes the shells off my nuts –
If you like em crunchy I have the right stuff.
Never bluff me!
Yo little nuts disgust me!
If they're pasty, yes, I'm tasty.
Roasting your nuts over an open fire,
I'm the object of your desire.

I am fire –
 Watch me burn –
  Wheel and come again like Saturn turns.
I knead your nuts.
I knead your nuts.
I knead your nuts.

"Sess" is a slang word for weed.

Where's My Period?

Miss Tough Love runs the school of life:
I failed her essay.
At the end of my sentence, I forgot my period.
My semi-colon was back spaced in my asterisk.
It got deleted, vid liquid paper, to prevent
Mistakes from happening.
My diction was legible.
My font was **bold** and was *italicized*.
I have read my script so many times:
It was double spaced with cursive lines.
I read it over,
And over,
And over,
And over!
Then
I submitted
My essay
Without
Having it proofread
The first sentence is the hardest to take:
Missing your period is the icing on the cake.
My first sentence was the following:
'I am woman enough'.
I forgot to put my period after that word 'enough.'
Proper punctuation –
Births liberation.
I failed the essay –
Due to my improper *parler*.
The school of life is tough.
My professor,
Miss Tough Love, was rough.
She introduced me
To hard times, repudiation, solitude,
Depression, unilateral matriarchy,
Rejection, alienation,
Endless ridicule, nocturnal hunger, homelessness, hopelessness,

Nausea,
Fear, hope, and insecurity –
Just because I forgot to type my period after typing the word
'enough.'
When you cannot think for yourself, others will think for you!
Ladies, wake up, wash your eyes, I implore you!
In Miss Tough Love's class,
I was class clown, so my peers kicked my ass.
Instead of feeling sorry for myself,
I was left all alone: Bell cut off my phone –
All I had was my poems.
No man would be my saviour:
I decided to work harder.
In Miss Tough Love's class:
Learning to be responsible is such a pain in the ass.
I had to work my butt off to survive:
At this point, I would do anything to stay alive.
I was a student, a janitor, and a secretary.
I brought apples to Miss Tough Love's desk.
My life was out of the ordinary.
In order
To get on Miss Tough Love's good side,
In order to survive.
One day, Miss Tough Love smiled.
She called me a good child.
I asked Miss Tough Love
If I could rewrite her essay.
Surprisingly, she obliged.
My new script started like this:
'I am woman enough to admit my mistakes.'
My final punctuation was the icing on the cake.
No more drama with commas or catastrophes with apostrophes!
My syllables were legible and not gullible.
Life put me on her honor roll.
Miss Tough Love held me in her arms.
It was nice to experience her charm.
My consciousness was karma.
I felt incredible, sassy, important, worthy of life, accepted, loved,

for myself –
Sheltered, satisfied, confident, and respectful of myself.
When you write your script
In Miss Tough Love's class,
Please
Make sure
To have it proofread
Before you submit it to her
If you forget to type your period
After the word, 'enough',
While writing your essay,
You might wind up sorry –
Or dead.
Period.

Ghettostocracy Redux

The poet is the true monarch of the ghetto:
The truth she speaks negates every veto.
Contradict her at your peril, for she vets
Every philosopher – and all the prophets.

III: Politricks

Why Keep Score?

Three million died in a Congo war:
A life is a life, so why keep score?

Soar above Victorian skies:
Hottentots taught their tots
Freedom cries.

United Nations, who are we?
Invisible witnesses to world catastrophes.

Human cumin, spicy food,
Treatable ills kill a mood.

Malnutrition thins out our world:
Toy meets boy, Helen meets Troy.

Die, if you do not see eye to eye,
With those who smog up the skies.
Cry, if your tears are dramatized
By lies the size of key-lime pies.

A spoonful of sugar helps the diabetes
Go round.
Glass-trimmed hovels grace shantytowns.
Ten cents, ten pence, suspends no sentence
The bull-faced cop yells.
Scents send tense spells.
Smell the coffee,
Smell well.

Prison is an industry
Needed
For corporate sodomy:
Greed.
Press rewind.

M.A.F.I.A.

Morte
Alla
Francia
Italia
Anela.

Death
To
France,
Italy
Screams.

Push For Peace

Push!
Shake your tush!
Make love, not war,
And shave your Bush!
I shaved my Bush like an American eagle:
Now it looks like Dr. Evil.
Push!
Shake your tush!
Make love, not war,
And shave your Bush!
I shaved my Bush like Kojak –
Now it's ready to attack.
Push!
Shake your tush!
Make love, not war,
And shave your Bush!
I shaved my Bush like Yul Brynner –
Now Saddam will eat it like *Kraft Dinner*.
Push!
Shake your tush!
Make love, not war,
And shave your Bush!
I shaved my Bush like a pig:
Now it needs to wear a wig.
Push!
Shake your tush!
Make love, not war,
And shave your Bush!
I shaved my Bush like *Mister Clean*:
Now it hums like a war machine.
Push!
Shake your tush!
Make love, not war,
And shave your Bush!

I shaved my Bush like Spider Man:
Now it has an action plan.
I shaved my Bush; it looks like Yoda.
Pray for peace and practice yoga.
Push!
Shake your tush!
Make love, not war,
And shave your Bush!
Push!
Shake your tush!
Make love, not war,
And shave your Bush!
I shaved my Bush like Pokémon –
To protest new wars inhuman.
Push!
Shake your tush!
Make love, not war,
And shave your Bush!
I shaved my Bush like Grover.
Don't you wish that the war was over?
Push!
Shake your tush!
Make love, not war,
And shave your Bush!
I shaved my Bush like Gandhi,
Shame on Bush, and pray for Condi?
Push!
Shake your tush!
Make love, not war,
And shave your Bush!

Say Word?

Why do women look so snappy-happy in maxi pad commercials?
Say word? Do they bleed at all during the dress rehearsals?
Indeed, this poem was created in the *Jheri Curl*-Free Zone:
Originality and versatility can never be cloned.
Limes are green, and I feel blue like the liquid –
Poured on a sanitary napkin, slapped in
Like a floral-scented tortilla.
On the second take, do they insert it back in again?
Come black again, in diverse shades of brown:
Change these funny commercials cos they make me frown.
Maxi pads lounge on receding pubic hairs:
Does any one out there really care?
Do you ever have that not-so-fresh feeling?
Do you ever have that toxic-shock feeling?

I Am Canadian, Dammit...

My morning ritual obliged me to rise
For the National Anthem.
"I am Canadian, I am proud,"
I sang in unison with my peers.
The bilingual chorus resonated
In my ears –
For years.
Oh Canada,
Terre de nos aïeux!
After singing, I was asked to be seated.
I commenced my day.
(I would now be illiterate if the teacher had had her way.)
Ton front est ceint
De fleurons glorieux.
Unintelligently, a moron
Would ask me:
"Where do you come from?"
I contemplated the idiot's ignorance
With indifference.
(Car ton bras sait porter l'épée!)
I called them incoherent.
To them I was a golliwog.
Because my hair was spongy like a bog;
I was a French Frog –
Locked in the jaws of a hog.
(Il sait porter la croix!)
I was
Born in Montréal,
Most *Canadien* city of them all.
I remember Terry Fox,
Victor Davis,
Pierre Elliott Trudeau –
(His son was a schoolmate of mine)
I remember when Trudeau lost to Joe Clark –
In 1979.
(Ton histoire est une épopée!)

I remember my many walks in Gatineau Park.
I remember Parliament Hill on Canada Day.
When Ben Johnson won gold –
(Des plus brilliants exploits…)
He was instantly Canadian.
When he lost, he was once-again Jamaican.
I remember the constitution in '82.
(Et ta valeur,)
The Mother-Fucking Tax and Free Trade…
Yeah, I remember that too.
(De foi trempée…)
I remember Nadia scoring a perfect ten
In the city where I was born –
Among Frenchmen.
Maestro Fresh Wes
Put Canadian hip hop on the map.
Michie Mee was in *Ladies First*!
So I give daps to rap.
I remember Oscar Peterson and all that Jazz.
I remember Haitian immigrants driving taxi cabs.
Mathieu Da Costa was a friend of mine.
He guided Champlain into Canada so…
Why wasn't his face ever on a dime?
I remember Marie Josèphe Angélique,
Shackled naked in Montreal.
Slavery existed in Canada
(Protégera nos foyers et nos droits…)
Even if historians don't recall.
"True, patriot love…"
What does that mean?
Why does being Black and Canadian seem obscene?
God has kept my heart "glorious and free."
Africadian soldiers fought in wars for liberty.
I am Canadian.
I am me.
(Protégera nos foyers et nos droits…)

Ladies First is a critique to sexism in rap in from Boogie Down Productions performed by femcees. Michie Mee was the only Canadian femcee star on that song. It featured icons such as MC Lyte, Monie Love and Queen Latifah.

Smart Black Girl

Smart Black girl
Articulate Black girl –
Quite able to think without a *Jheri-Curl*.
If this is so true, why can't I rule the world?
Why should my skin tone deem me a simpleton?
When the moon gives way to those clad with melanin.
My voice scares you because I rage war:
My mental altitude propels me to soar.
My wit is ill: I never ever quit.
The corn-rows in my hair are extra legit.
When I speak, you are amazed:
Believe it or not, there were white slaves –
Not Kunta Kente, but Billy Jo Bob –
Chased out of Africa by livid Black mobs.
My wit astounds you; yes, I am sharp!
Snowmen never ever swim with sharks!

Hieroglyphs were not a myth:
The Chem in my phlegm makes me a physicist.

IQ

Intellectual Quotient:
Kosher?
No, sir!
Can it determine Intelligence?
Hell, no?
Does it segregate?
Does wind blow?

Montague and Jensen
Have taught me a lesson,
In anthropology of
African dystrophy and philosophy.
Know all your history, and nothing less:
You'll pass every test.
Confess...

Quotient means to divide:
Quod vide.
La suite de mes idées
Coincide.
Cerebrums are boundless:
How can IQ tests count this?
The trigonometry of my mind.

Leaves my third eye blind.
Reading a book...
Does not make you smart.
Life is a lesson, life is an art.
Life is an artist –
Creating art.

A scribe can tell
That IQ testing
Was dreamt up in hell.
Intelligence, practicality...
Prognosis: abnormality,

Tortures my family
With intellectual brutality.

My apathy stems from being Black and morose:
Lemme pass dis stupid test with my eyes closed.

Dead Man Walking

Once upon an eve, he was chillin with thieves.
They lurked about in a moonlight serenade
Amongst dry leaves.

Like a duck in a pond, he swam to the shore,
Unaware of what hurt dirty waters can have in store.
Ecologically speaking, his lovemaking equated dreaming:
If geysers spat water, then his well was leaking.

His flow endured a current, so strong and so unpure,
Lo and behold, it struck a kind Moor.

She was the river and Oshun was her name.
Inside her he quivered, he grunted, and he came.
Pulsations, like malice, would rattle and hum.
As intelligent as he was, he forgot his condom.

Pain was plausible; death's chariot was his new apostle.
Hostile like a fossil, so charred and so numb,
Jonquils had pistils that shot with a vengeance.
His phallus, like Dallas, was used like a gun.

In the name of fun he died in her arms.
Nymphs and white shadows recruited his charms.
Killing him softly was the name of her song.
She poisoned his jockeys while he donged her thongs.

Her apothecary was dismal, her demands were physical.
Her beauty belittled intelligence with riddles.
If his tender vittles had fled her cat,
He'd have had an acquittal, and that's a fact.
Since his hung jury inflicted pain,
Rest in peace, dead man walking,
I'll remember your name.

Flip Your Wig

Flip your wig!
You're ashamed of your hair!
So you ignite the
Sick stench of burning hair.
Wake up, wake up!
Your lye is lying –
Your soul is dying,
Because you're ashamed of your
African Flair.
You put gloves on your hands,
Relaxer on your scalp.
You need no chemicals!
Your head needs no fake help.

Osmosis perforates your head of state:
It disables your ability to handle mental debates.
Harriet Tubman had no perm:
She never went to school, but she was well-learned.
Sojourner had no conk, just freedom's songs:
Was her hair long?
Assata was right though she was wronged –
Her hair signaled that she was strong.

Angela's fro was like the sun.
Run niggers, run niggers! Yo niggers run!
Be weave me when I say that you deceive me –
Why must a horse go tailless for "*Cali* dreaming?"
Know that *Barbie*'s "pretty hair" was made in Taiwan –
Her vagina in China,
And her ass in Hong Kong.
Cherubic kids with big blue eyes and blonde hair –
Make you want to lose your African flair,
Blue-eyed, pretty-faced, and beaming –
White dolls have always been deceiving.
Have you ever tried to cornrow *Barbie*'s hair?
It just shrivels and starts to disappear...

Chucky was the doll I should have kept.
If you're *Jheri-Curl* free, let's take it to the left.
Hair relaxer is corrosive and is gravely abrasive.
Why, you put it on your scalp
With gloves!
Since hair relaxer is aggressive –
Come on, let's face it –
Kiddie perm is sure to burn.
(Tender heads want to learn.)
Relaxer stinks; it reeks like cabbage.
Scalps ravaged,
Brains damaged…
But I'm an African, not a savage.
Flip your wig!
You're ashamed of your hair!
Betray your roots and be prepare to die,
Due to the lie of lye –
Unprepared.

Word Up!

In the beginning was the word "man."
His syllable was pivotal, and then came a woman.
Adam's rib was the staircase to heaven.
The number of days it took to build the world was seven.
Heptadecimal thoughts concurred –
The Good Word was never heard.
Man is here to serve, that was the plan,
Set in holy stone in a Judaic land.
Woolly-haired God struck poetry with a rod:
All who deceived him were turned to sod.

If Mary's Eyes Were Blue

If Mary's eyes were blue…
If Mary's eyes were blue,
And if Mary's hair were blonde,
Do you really think that a Roman
Soldier would have told her to run along –
With a bun in her oven some nine months gone?

If Mary's eyes were blue,
And if Mary's hair were blonde,
She would've been lodged in the *Hilton*,
And not in a "manger" on a lawn –
With a bun in her oven some nine months gone!

If Mary's eyes were blue,
And if Mary's hair were blonde,
Whites would sun themselves on a cloud –
Blacks in hotels would not be allowed –
Despite buns in our ovens some nine months gone!

Mary's eyes weren't blue:
They were jet, they were black:
She was a Black Madonna,
Prima Donna, that's a fact.
If Jerusalem is to the east –
They came from the west.
They followed the star from Africa.
(I'm good in Geography, I know best.)
Jesus is not blue-eyed;
Jesus has a fro!
Don't brainwash me with your B.S. "Bible Studies"
Or I'll tell you where to go.

Mary's eyes were not blue.
Mary's hair was not blonde.
That is why a Roman soldier told her to run along –
With a bun in her oven with some nine months gone!

The World Is Yours

The world is yours:
Take it in the palm of your hands.
Before you shape it –
Make a plan.
Pattie cake, pattie cake, baker's man:
Shape your world as best as you can.

Never sit in a situation
Full of fuss and frustration.

Words are real.
How do you feel?
The power of words
Can make you heal.
Some people make mistakes:
You know the deal!

Conflict resolution
Can cause a revolution.

Shape your world, boys and girls!
Let your verses rock this world!

The world is yours.
Take it in the palms of your hands.
Before you shape it –
Make a plan.
Pattie cake, pattie cake, baker's man:
Shape your world as best as you can.

Do you lose or win?
Do you sink or swim?
Do you want out?
Or do you want in?

Raise your voices, make positive choices.
Look towards the future, love and nurture.
The continuation of history starts with you:
Celebration starts with you...

The world is yours.
Take it in the palms of your hands.
Before you shape it –
Make a plan.
Pattie cake, pattie cake, baker's man:
Shape your world as best as you can.

We all feel pain, grief, sorrow:
What about tomorrow?
Do you lead or do you follow?
Individuality is your key.
If you know the words,
Repeat after me:

The world is yours.
Take it in the palms of your hands.
Before you shape it –
Make a plan.
Pattie cake, pattie cake, baker's man:
Shape your world as best as you can.

Stranger Fruit

Strange fruits grow on trees,
Pollinated by killer bees –
Depleted by disease,
Full of worms and fleas at ease.
Strange fruits fall to the ground –
With a sound stronger than *Dolby Surround*.
Strange fruits, mangled by hounds,
Get exported in maggot-ridden mounds.
Strange fruits stolen from the store,
Get put on sale, but are ignored.
I ate a mango without its peel,
I loved the way it made me feel.
Mango, I come, without pain –
Tropical fruits need sun and rain.
Jack frost kills fruit by dulling their roots;
Cops crush Black boys under black jackboots.
Chlorophyll and stagnant piss –
Emulate gorillas in the mist.
To Billie Holiday, I raise my BLACKPHIST –
And it goes a little something like this....
Mist...

Mist

The mist from the Nile
Is denial from vinyl.
Divine are all the rhymes
Branded invalid and wild.
Bliss is dismissed in the mist.
Like piss, find all the rhymes
That project my fist.

What Happened To Michael Jackson?

My son asked me:
"Mommy, what happened to Michael Jackson?
Will I be white like him when I grow up?"
I said: "Don't be silly, son. Let me pour some hot history in your cup.
Whites tan to look black, some of them get perms:
Blacks lighten their skin and straighten their hair in return.
The Hottentot Venus had a bootie so sublime,
It inspired the bustle during Victorian times.

Queen Victoria had a ghetto bootie!
Even Queen Charlotte was an African cutie –
But Charlottetown in painted white.

The Queen Charlotte Islands are on the West Coast, right?
Bo Derek made braids and beads very trendy.
(Europeans never like to voice their Negro envy.)

We all have the same Black mother."

Sisters and brothers…
If intelligence is Hellenic, give it a twenty-one-gun salute.
Napoleon and Champollion played the same tin flute.
Anthony and Cleopatra were an interracial pair,
Waaaaaaay before *Jungle Fever* ever hit the air.
The hot-comb created the first Black woman millionaire.
Flip your "Whig" and reject your African flair.
If you were told that –
mulatto, chocolato, light-skinned, *noir*, African, tar baby, piss-yella, hi-yella, kushite, marabou, *pied-noir*, red-skinned, half-breed, pink-toe, *coolie*, Black and White, caramel-colored, mocha-colored, jigaboo, sambo, colored, red-skinned, blackie, Black Irish, *métisso, garifuna, dundus*, red-bone, *grimo*, almost-white, not-quite-white, *moolie*, not black-enough, too black, Irish nigger, ethnic-type, SP**OO**K, Black Apache, blackie, jungle bunny, *négresse*, darkie, coon, Mandingo, *Black-chiney*, Black Irish,

negro, *café au lait*, blue-black, mixed, oreo, bi-racial, fraction
person, brown-skinned, *Latino*, octoroon, maroon, spade, nigger,
Nubian, *pétion*, sand-nigger, quadroon, Creole, blackamoor, etc –
Mean black,
Then you, too, would be a little confused: even *Crayola* knows
that.
Black is a political term; Michael Jackson got himself a political
perm.
No one is perfectly black, no one is perfectly white.
A hexadecimal colour code will prove me right.
Some folks are melanin def', while others are melanin deficient.
A tan in a can is seldom efficient:
Magazines, and "hollyweird" try to make black colours nonexist-
ent.
They will not cast thee, if you look black and "ghastly."
Nose jobs are recommended for you to be a star. See…
Lighter skin is in, so is proper *parler*...
If you are from the ghetto and want real pay,
Most employers will say: "*No way, José!*"
"We want an Ofay!"
Some Blacks play obscure in order to white appear.
The fear of a black planet *really* is their scare.

Methinks that Michael Jackson really knows this.
The melting pot is piping hot; yeah, but it's still full of racists.

IV: Afromatrix

Black Madonna

Avé to you, Madonna, and to Yahvé.
Black Madonna, Belladonna,
It is to you that I pray,
A praying mantis in the grass,
Shackled and clasped,
Who grasped the essence (grasped as incense),
Of your mysterious past.
"La Morenata," the little dark one,
Implies that you are a *negrita,* thus kissed by the sun.
Iconoclasts fear you; so near you, I live.
Mother Earth, dark as dirt, life is what you give.
You are:
Statuesque, Romanesque, here replicated as a fresco.
I revere your silhouette with a poetic arabesque.

My prose is dedicated to a Nubian rose
With Kemetic Venus hairs, wry and superposed.
Our Lady is Black, that beautiful godly black.
Revered in Spain, France, Czechoslovakia,
And in other countries oddly Black.
You are Isis, Magdalena, Sarah, and Mary.
The fact that they paint you white
Is, to me, very scary.

Avé, Black Matriarch!
Avé, Queen of Spades!
Avé, Mother Supreme!
How dare fools make you a slave!

Once A Month I Suffer From Cultural PMS

I'm a black-bilingual technologist.
What do you mean?
I do exist; let me be a part of your team.
Negative attitudes give me cramps
Advil cannot cure.
Let me tell you about some of the things that I endure.
Once a month, I suffer from cultural PMS.
I get cramps from ignorance.
I experience mood swings when people
Pester me about where I'm from.
Once a month, I suffer from cultural PMS.

The other day, I was in the elevator after work.
And this lady asks me: "Where do you come from?"
I said: "I come from the 11th floor!"
The lady asks me again: "Where do you come from?"
I said: "I come from upstairs, the 11th floor,
And you come from downstairs, you come from the fifth floor!"
Once a month I suffer from cultural PMS!

Diversity is about everything we do.
It's about me and it's about you,
And you know it's true.
Diversity is in constant evolution
That is part of a solution
That could uplift this nation.
Once a month I suffer from cultural PMS.

Diversity is my personal flavour –
It's my unique style that works in my favour.
We all have different views
That need to be respected
Because all come in different hues.
Once a month I suffer from cultural PMS.

Don't frikkin ask me if I only eat spicy food!
Or if I like it here: Yes, I hear that too!
Get your nasty dirty hands out of my natural hair!
Respect my space! Damn! Be fair!
You make my Afro want to take a vacation.
Ignorant folks like you need cultural meditation.
When you ask me: "Oni, is it true what they say about black men?"
My answer to you is, "Yes they are intelligent, and they make excellent friends!"
Once a month I suffer from cultural PMS.

I want to be a part of a team that shares my dreams.
I want to be a leader, I want the green.
Society lacks creative solutions.
Diversity is inspirational, it's a revolution.

Once a month I suffer from cultural PMS,
This is an issue I would like to address.

Hail, Mary, Full Of Grace

Hail, Mary, full of grace –
Wipe the tears off my face.
I'll pray seven times
To dissolve my sins!
Seven chimes for seven winds;
Seven seas for seven days;
Seven riddles for seven knaves;
Seven songs, seven poems,
Seven gods; I promise to know them:
*Shango, Damballah, Legba, Agoué, Petro
Erzalie* and *Yanvalou.*
At seven zero seven, hear my plea –
The clock struck past the seventh hour:
Seven ticks and seven showers;
Seven kisses and adorations,
Seven reverences for your creation.

Blackness

Blackness: shines, defines, Shaka Shakur
Strong history, wilding, misery! Slavery,
Bravery. Stand Proud, aloud in a crowd,
Teach, preach, reach
Blackness!

Belle Femme Noire

Sensuality is projected by my presence.
My duality has been grasped.
My soul is perfected.
My tears are liquid glass.
Primary colours glisten.
Copycats try to mimic my splendour.
My beauty gets stolen by fashion vendors.
Can I escape the madness that greets me daily?
When my beauty is only praised when plied by a pale lady.

This is my time, my place; I am a diva with no face.
My endless curves finish in a knot at my elbows.
My mind can race to places that only God knows.
I have the right to be narcissistic:
Even the petals of my pain are fantastic.
A jonquil's pistil teases me, poison ivy pleases me.
Love me, love me not: My Garden of Eden has had a drought.
My likes are rare,
Birthing beauty to spite despair.

I am the Hottentot Venus, hot sex on a platter.
My fro is my crown and my shadow is my sceptre.

My Afro

On a sunny day, my Afro
Was my hat under the shade.
Bright lights and honeybees
Were floating in the breeze.
Pomade
Fell like a cranial cascade,
Hair food –
Soul food.
My curls dangle in the shade:
My coils needed
An oily serenade.

Black Women's History

Fed only bread and water,
She has given birth in cotton fields.
She has children who have no father.

Soul Rebel

There is too much hate to articulate.
Volatile moods are detected:
Gesticulate!
Men don't care if a pretty woman is crazy –
As long as their peckers peak.
Download super freaks!
Who has the magic stick?
Naked all day in bed,
Eating yogurt and watching kung fu movies –
Then you enter my life to thank me for my kindness.
Your third eye has blindness.
Tripping over the many pages of signatures before mine...

If your features are very strong,
Feel empowered by your favorite song.
Stay beautiful, accept nothing less from life!
I wear the black of the night on my sleeves.
I'm fashionable:
When you think of me, feel relieved
Cause I'm a Soul Rebel.
One for the bass, two for the treble.
Today, I feel more empowered then I did yesterday –
Wild women like me sing the blues.
Like armadillos in red panties –
Soon to be road kill –
Wild women like me
Will bend even saints to our will –
To give our children, the children of Mother Earth, the bright
future we quill.
I'm a
Soul Rebel.

I am erotic; you call me neurotic:
I could never be a genius since I do not have a penis.
Empowered women like me are dangerous:
We set the boundaries of your existence.

We are Soul Rebels.
Women like us are drawn to the occult.
We are fashionable,
Wearing the black of the night on our sleeves –
And the blue of the day on our thongs –
Serving an extra helping of sex,
To make the human race survive,
Via a heaping serving of healthy breasts and thighs –
We make soul babies.

I am a Soul Rebel
One for the bass, two for the treble.

Playing strip poker like a reformed smoker –
I'm the Queen of Spades, not the joker.
Empowered women like me are dangerous.
We are the flowers of your souls in bloom
Burning with desire,
We choose.
Smell our perfume
Stay beautiful... Accept nothing less from life!
Be a Soul Rebel.
One for the bass, two for the treble.

Like the truly holy,
Stir up trouble.

V: Poet Talks

Yo Soy Oni Luciano

Cubans await release; Haitians still detained.
I am Haitian, I am Cuban, and I feel black pain.
Yo soy Oni Luciano

Yo soy una mujer de dos islas...
Call me *Haitiando*
Mwen se fanm de peyi.
Big up, Cuba and Haiti!
Immigration and Naturalization
Won't set me free.
Yo soy, Oni Luciano:
La mariposa negra –
Una negrita linda –
Nou la, nou led,
Sak pase?
Kampe Red!
If the Atlantic were blue
Now it's red...
Bled...
And she bled and she bled and she bled and she bled...
7 days at sea trying to reach Miami –
Overloaded Haitian boats filled with my family.
Yo soy, Oni Luciano
Un sabor cubano en la poesia haitiana –
In *Kreyol, y ingles,* it sounds so dope.
Otra vez!
God bless the little girl in the Yellow dress...
Bled...
And she bled and she bled and she bled and she bled...
When I come back, I want to go home.
Old Haitian policy contradicts democracy.
O Dios! Hypocrisy, is it the land of the free?
Not even *Jheri-Curl*-free, nobody is home-free.
Mwen se fanm de peyi,
Big up Cuba and Haiti!
Immigration and Naturalization

Won't set me free.
Yo soy, Oni Luciano.
Perpetual detention, water retention,
Racial profiling inspires free styling.
Why am I smiling?
Papers need filing.
Yo soy, Oni Luciano
No puedo bailar. No puedo cantar. Me siento mal. No puede vivir.
Viva la libertad. Mi gente es verdad.
Anacaona is super bad

I can't live without my poetry
My poetry
Yo soy, Oni Luciano…

Anacaona means "Golden Flower" in Arawak. Anacaona was the first Haitian
Queen. Born in Léogane, Haiti, she ruled the island of Hispaniola with poems
called *Aryetos* – war poems.

I'm A Poetic Shit Disturber

Charge this poetic shit disturber with lyrical murder!
I don't take shit! Let's take this matter further.
I don't play; I have my say, my opinion counts.
Seize the day! *Carpe diem!*
Poetic requiems analyze the lies my eyes see per diem.
I will rock you with poetic mayhem.
I'm a black sheep: no I don't blend!
Status quo is for average Joes.
Jails come in all shapes and sizes.
Feel my flow.
Fix the disrespect! Introspect! This is Oni, in full effect.
I'm here to inspect the direct foolishness of all the defects.
Hear this, I'm not playing!
No, I'm not insane, but I remain –
True to my words, I'm a social critic:
Life is a speed bag, that's why I hit it.
Two thumbs down with a lyrical frown,
Get in my way you feel a take-down,
The breakdown is what I write.
Public Enemy says
"Don't believe the hype."
Feast your eyes and glut your soul –
My Canadian orature will soon unfold.
I'm bold, I have balls of brass:
If you don't like it, I'll kick your ass.

Who Gives a Flux?

Who gives a flux about what I think?
I flow with the wind,
The rain offers me a drink.
Flux yourself, and flock real high.
An influx of flexibility can make my head touch my thigh.
Flux these fluxing institutions and what they fluxing think.
Flux like prostitution! Who said that life was fluxing pink?
Flux *la vie en rose*, and let me tell you *quelque chose*:
"I don't give a flipping flux about what you think of my fluxing
prose!"
Flux with me, and I'll flux you up.
My fluxing flowery flowetry is fluxing serious, and it has fluxing
clout.
Too many fluxing phony phonies out there claim that they are
fluxing ripe.
I'm fluxing lyrically imbalanced, and my fluxing rhymes are
fluxing tight!
If I could flux, a good flux good, how much good hood can I good
flux good.
If I could flux a good flux good, the hood I would flux would be a
good flux!
Ugggh....
I'm the best poetic, diva flux that you ever, fluxing had!
Even my fluxing kindergarten teacher will tell you that I was so
fluxing bad.
Fluxing sperm donors should never flux with the fluxing word,
"dad."
If I got any fluxing child support payments, I'd be so fluxing glad.
I treat fluxing metaphors like fluxing whores, like a fluxing lyrical
pimp.
My verbal influorescence will flux you up like a fluxing imp.
Have you ever fluxed forcefully in a fluxing metal staircase,
And put an element of shock and fluxing delight on your fluxing
lover's fluxed-up face?
Fluxing with me is like fluxing the icing on the fluxing cake!
Daps to those who have fluxed in a fluxing public place:

One for the fluxing treble, and two for the motherfluxing bass.
All I want to do is turn this fluxing poetic Motherfluxer out –
Only the fluxing funky Motherfluxers know what I'm really
fluxing talking about.
I can never talk like a fluxing sailor since I'm a fluxing, sophisti-
cated lady.
All the fluxing pseudo-fathers out there should fluxing take care
of their babies.
Who gives a flux about what I think?
It's fluxing acid raining outside...
So I will pour myself a drink.
Flux *la vie en rose*, who said that life was fluxing pink?
Flux cockblockers, I'm fluxing multi-orgasmic and I'm fluxing
cataclysmic.
Ever since I performed in the *Vagina Monologues*, my fluxing
pussy is fluxing

Algorithmic.

Nfokuz

Look at me! Focus!
I am the first flower of spring,
The crocus.
I burst through the
Whitest of whitest of snows,
Before the groundhog casts its shadow.
"The eyes are the windows of the soul":
My eyes are a prismic beauty to
Behold.
Eyes, they never grow old as they capture
Treasures as precious as gold.
I am a scribe. With my eyes,
I inscribe lyrics, text,
Both concave and convex.
My eyes have been passed down to me from my extensive
And expensive ancestry.
My eyes belonged to beggars,
Thieves, to the politically unrelieved,
To kings and to queens.
My eyes have seen many things –
Both beautiful and obscene.
My eyes are fiends capturing the rapture
Of truth.
My eyes are demons –
Broken down from the DNA found in semen.
My eyes are heathens.
My eyes have seen rape; my eyes are wisdom.
I am an artist and, with my eyes,
I create
From my vision.
My eyes have seen glory.
My eyes have seen the curvilinear
Lines of my story.
If you borrowed my eyes, you would see history.
Ain't mine eyes seen the glory
Of the coming of the Lord?

After slavery – all that horror –
My eyes flash and slash like a sword.

Iambic Pain

My love for poetry causes me to sing iambic pain,
Sonatas submersed with sextants in the sun,
Was this the place that lynched a thousand men?
Was this the love that flinched the son of Kam?
Meters...
Meters...
Meters...
Drunken
With unaccented,
Gullible syllables,
Submitted to surrender
Their souls –
Submitted to surrender
Their souls –
Submitted to surrender
Their souls.
Two times two,
Four times one,
Zero plus four,
Quatuors –
Treating metaphors like whores,
Treating metaphors like whores,
Treating metaphors like whores:
Quatuors...
Pain was iambic, Shakespeare was a cur.
Moors are not bandits,
Some are misunderstood.
Robin Hood was cool –
Trotting on minions rule –
Follow the thread, if you are a spool,
Weave your thoughts in iambic pain!
Words are not crazy; you're insane.

Please Pay The Poet

Poets make the most money
When they die.
Some poets make you laugh, some poets
Make you cry.
Some poets make you angry, some poets make you think.
Poets make you wise –
And yet poets are still radicalized.
Poets are always expected to perform for free –
To read for free, to work for free –
Since poets "don't need money to be."
Poets are social critics, poets are sociologists.
Some poets need toxicologists.
Poets are historians, poets are teachers.
Poets are sly, poets are preachers.
Poets are cynical, poets are analytical,
Poets are critical, poets are lexical.
Poets are political, so politicians quote poets –
So does the rest of society, and most of us know it.
No one wants to pay the poet, since the poet is humble:
This is how the poetic cookie crumbles.
Poets need to get paid since they, too, have social needs.
Poets have obligations: poets perform deeds.
Poets need funding; poets have a vision.
Poets, and you know it, are here on a mission.
Please, pay the poet! Poets have a price!
Poets make a constant sacrifice.
Please pay the poet!

Metaphors

Metaphors are whores:
I pimp verses, embedded
Lies, tongue-agile, wet.

Shout Outs

Hail, Mary. *Avé Maria, Je vous salue Marie.* I want to thank the creator and my ancestors for giving me the ability to express the communication of my inner dialogue via poetry. Honneur-Respect. I'm eternally grateful to my angels. My angels wear combat gear and they are all around me.

Much love and appreciation to McGilligan Books: Ann, thank you for publishing my work and for believing in me, Zoë et Lisa, thank you all for your hard work and for seeing *Ghettostocracy* through, thank you for your patience – *merci, ampil.* Thank you to my editor-lyrical architect-amazing-mentor-superhero, Dr. George Elliott Clarke. Whooo George, I feel all grown up now! Dear Lillian Allen, and Afua Cooper, thanks for the "push" and for the encouragement. Klyde Broox, *Jah Bless, My Best Friend is White* too, thank you for the jokes on St. Clair Avenue. John W. MacDonald has a beautiful spirit and he's a "supa bad" dude. Thank you for the photos! Danilo, thank you for making *Ghettostocracy* look *très* sexy, I'm so happy with my first book!

I want to thank my whole family – my parents for giving me life. I want to thank my mother for pushing me damn hard to be the best I could be (this made me **very, very, very** crazy at times). I want to thank my brothers for being the best brothers that any sister could ask for. I want to thank my sons for being my best friends – and for the good times (my youngest son Toussaint's first word was James Brown). I want to thank my grandmother for teaching me how to hustle with my twelve fingers (I was born with bilateral polydactyly), and how to kick ass. My grandmother knew *savate;* she had a serious round house kick, and front jab – *grand-mère* administered a deadly... *a Haitian-Cuban time-out.*

So many people have supported me through the years, and if I leave out any names by accident, I still love you – you know who you are. George, thank you for being an inspiration and for being there for me. I want to thank Brother Oji and MACPRI for getting me on stage first. I want to thank Jane Anido, Alan Neal, Julie Delaney, and to the CBC for getting my poetry to the first CBC Poetry Face-Off, *a mari usque ad mare,* when people did not know what the hell Slam poetry was. Thank you to all my fans.

To Nestus, Nadia, Mummy Burke, Valdyne Limage, Sandra and Jacqueline Beaugé, thank you for getting me out of *The Dragon's Lair*.

To *my homegurls and homeboys,* Darashani Joachim, Benetta Standly, Sibi Cole, Lieann Koivukoski, Richard Naster, Barbie Shore, Maria Hawkins, Toivo Koivukoski, Garmamie Sideau (YEH), Ken Birchall, Tremaine Loadholt, BLACKPHIST, Paul Symes, Ross May, Donna Williams, Dave, Suzanne and Gentle Stavanger, André Perrier, OCISO, Graham Nunn, Carlos Perez, Catherine Zytfeld Macdonald, Steve Zytfeld, Alex Munter, Amanda Graham, Jessica Carfagnini, Andre Michael Bölten, Kersten Klenter, Byron Kocen, Mary Nash, Sandy Sharkey, Adrian Ulysses, Katherine Watson, Maggie Joseph, Mike Frier, Tachelle Wilkes, Shauntay Grant, Monica Williams, Paule Mercier, Jeremy Dias, Suzanne Harding, The V-Day Ottawa 2006 cast & crew, SASC, Erin Lee-Todd, Karen Morin, Winston Bell, Gillian Graham, Lorna Tate, Desy and Joanie Doran, Marina Dooley, Brandon Lee, Radana, Debra Dunlop, Warren Layberry, Shelley Taylor, Catherine Nicholson, Maura Volante, Jodi Durnin, Don Hewson, Ann Khalil, Jay Macintosh, Michel-Ange Hippolyte, Janice Reid, Mitch Stone, Ana Karyn Garcia-and to "The Angels," Maurice McIlwain, Oriana Macedo, Nalo Hopkinson, Jennifer McTavish, Mother Tongue Books, Irene Viel, Eric Dubeau, Jay Pitter, Fatima Diop, thank you, for loving me like your sister, always. Michael Franti, thank you for reaching out to me in an unforgettable way, for showing me "something beautiful" and for *Every Single Soul*, Fateema Sayani, "Black On Black" – thank you beautiful sisters, CHUO, CKCU, John W. MacDonald, Sue Fergueson, Allan Wigney, Taloua, Sabine Daniel, Jill Brogan, Centretown News, CTV, John Ruttle, Paul Wing, Library and Archives Canada, Eric Longley, Joel Haslam, *The Ottawa Xpress*, CJOH, Randall Ware, Pauline Portelance, *The Ottawa Citizen*, *The Ottawa Sun*, *Metro Ottawa*, and to all media who have helped me promote my work, and to The Canada Council for the Arts, The Ottawa International Writers Festival, The Ontario Arts Council, MASC, The Dub Poets Collective… to everyone who has ever given me a mic and a stage to perform on…

Thank you!
Oni the Haitian Sensation

About The Author

Oni – the Haitian Sensation – is Ottawa's poetry diva, an internationally recognized slam poetry champion and an ambassador for arts and education. Her award-wining poetry workshops on HIV/AIDS were featured in *Macleans Magazine*. She has been commissioned to write poetry for organizations such as the Canadian Commission for UNESCO, the CBC, the Bytowne Museum, and for Ottawa's Winterlude Festival. In 2005, Oni was the headlining poet at the Queensland Poetry Festival in Australia.

Oni directed Canada's first National Poetry Slam competition, the Canadian Spoken Worldlympics. She is the first Canadian woman to tour the European Slam poetry circuit, and in 2002, she was the first curator of Slam Poetry for the Ottawa International Writers Festival. Oni is the founder of Ottawa's longest running poetry slam and she created Ottawa's first national slam poetry team at the Ottawa Fringe Festival. *Ottawa Xpress Magazine* readers voted Oni the best poet in Ottawa. She completed York University, Faculty of Education, Faculty of Fine Arts and the Ontario Arts Council Artist in Education Certificate. She graduated from Algonquin College's Interactive Multimedia and Web Specialist programs and has her Macromedia Certification.

A single parent with three young children, Oni is a social activist who is concerned with domestic violence, literacy, racism, diversity, bullying, and AIDS awareness. In 2004, Oni created Ottawa's first public forum on HIV/AIDS for the African Caribbean Community. She was nominated for the YWCA Women of Distinction Award; is on the Board of Directors of the Ottawa Women's Credit Union and of the Canadian Tribute to Human Rights. Oni the Haitian Sensation works as a freelancer and she can be reached at www.mesooni.com.